Self-Discovery Journal for Women:

365 Days of Magical Lists for Happiness, Gratitude, and Everyday Bliss

Dreamstorm Publications

Hello Gorgeous!

Please give yourself a big round of applause...

No, really. Do it! Get on your feet and give yourself a round of Oscar-night worthy applause, a big pat on the back, pop-your-own-damn-collar kind of vibe.

Know why?

By choosing this book, you've decided to create one of the most worthwhile and life-changing habits ever – daily journaling. But this journal is not just about sitting down and writing endlessly. It's creating lists that will help you to get your goals, dreams and aspirations in order.

Why is this such a big deal?

You may have heard this before...an unwritten goal is just a wish. No lies there! So, if you get up every day wishing that someday you're going to lose some weight, start eating healthy, spend more time with the family, go back to school, stop smoking or whatever but you never actually do anything, then this is a great first step towards achieving what you want in life. In here, you can write down what you want out of life and start holding yourself accountable.

How can I benefit from keeping a daily journal?

Aside from keeping track of your goals, there are also many other benefits to making these daily lists. Whether you're a creative person at heart and you just want an outlet to record your thoughts and ideas, or if you're stressed and need somewhere to organize your thoughts into clear, easy-to-understand segments without the possible judgement and lack of confidentiality that often comes with confiding in others, writing a daily list journal is a worthwhile avenue.

Quick Tips to Make the Habit Stick:

Yes, keeping a daily list journal might be a daunting prospect for many, and you've probably started feeling the writer's block creeping down your shoulders and into your fingertips already. Don't worry – with fresh new writing inspirations and prompts every day for the next 365 days, you won't find yourself wondering what to write about on any given day. Starting any new habit can be difficult at first, but here are some quick tips that will help make journaling a seamless part of your everyday life:

- *Choose a specific time of day to write.* The best times are when you've just woken up in the morning or right before you go to bed. But don't feel constrained by those times. Once you feel the urge to write, simply grab your pen and start pouring your heart into those pages

- Don't worry about errors or how it looks, that's just cosmetic. *Instead, be yourself with no makeup or filter on.* Write what's in your heart –your journal is one place that you'll face no judgement or censure and you don't have to keep up any appearances.

- *Find somewhere you feel comfortable in mind and body.* So, whether it's in your bed, the breakfast nook, a little corner of your closet…go there and write.

365 Days of Magical Lists for Self-Discovery, Gratitude, and Everyday Bliss

Your Personal Space:

Vision board or inspirational photos. Your choice.

Your Personal Space:
Vision board or inspirational photos. Your choice.

Day 1 __/__/__

Reasons to Celebrate: It's the first day of a new life-changing habit! That, of course, is enough reason to celebrate. Whether it's your actual birthday or not, let's pop some champagne or at least a glass of sparkling water and *make a note of five (5) gifts that we have to be thankful for in 201X*. Here are some suggested categories to get you started: Home & Family, Love, Friendship, Growth, Health.

Day 2 __/__/__

Breaking Bad Habits: Sometimes we try to fix everything we think is wrong with our lives in just one go. That often ends with us biting off more than we can chew – so let's set some bite-sized goals to get the year started. All you have to do is answer one question: *What is one bad habit that you'd like to break this year, and how are you going to do it?*

You will never change your life, until you change something you do daily.
-*Unknown*

Day 3 __/__/__

Morning Music: What's on your Playlist? Music can definitely get you in the mood for a great day! *What ten songs are on your playlist for that early-morning jam session on your way to work?*

Day 4 __/__/__

Here's to a Dream Vacation in _____! Fill in the blank – name one vacation spot that's at the top of your bucket list. Now, here are a few more blanks to fill in…

Why do you want to go to _____?
What are the top three places you'll visit when you get to _____?
How much will the trip to _____ cost?
When would you like to take the trip to _____?
Who would you like to go to _____ with?

The world is a book; those who don't travel read only a page.
-St. Augustine

Day 5 __/__/__

What are you biggest time-wasters? Very often, we put off the things we have to do things that are just a waste of time. It's the art of procrastination. Jot down a list of your biggest time-wasters below

Day 6 __/__/__

What I learned today… Every day is a new opportunity to learn something new, whether you planned to or not. *What was today's lesson for you?*

Live as if you were to die tomorrow. Learn as if you were to live forever.
-Mahatma Gandhi

Day 7 __/__/__

My Manifesto. Do you have a set of words, beliefs, promises that you live by? *Write your personal manifesto or mission statement here.*

Day 8 __/__/__

Build it into Being. Build your dream home word-by-word today. *Describe every square foot in as much detail as you can manage.* Got drawing skills? Bring it to life with a quick rough sketch.

If you don't build your dreams, someone else will hire you to build theirs.
-Tony Gaskins

Day 9 __/__/__

Staycation Ideas! Planning a staycation? Make a quick note of all the top spots you'd like to visit in your hometown or city.

Day 10 __/__/__

Myself as an Author... Ever felt like you could write a book? Think up at least three possible titles for books you would write and include a short blurb on what they're about.

Books are uniquely portable magic.
-Stephen King

Day 11 __/__/__

Pen Down Those Pet Peeves! Everyone has some things they just can't stand. Scribble down your worst pet peeves.

Day 12 __/__/__

Take me there (in my dreams). You've probably read about this place, or seen it in a movie – but in your heart, you've been there a million times. *What fictional place would you love to visit or even live in, and list three (3) reasons why.*

To those who can dream, there is no such place as far away.
-Unknown

Day 13 __/__/__

Ready, Set, Jet! Never know what to pack for a trip? Jot down a list of your must-have travel items and save it for that trip you're going on soon, *wink*!

Day 14 __/__/__

Failures and Lessons. Failure is as much a part of life as victory. Make a list of five (5) things you've ever failed at, and what you learnt from them.

Failure is a bruise, not a tattoo.
-Jon Sinclair

Day 15 __/__/__

Some Advice to Ignore. Not all advice is good advice. Pick your memory for some of the worst pieces of advice you've ever received and why it was so bad.

Day 16 __/__/__

You've Got Skills! Make a list of three (3) things you're really good at.

When love and skill work together, expect a masterpiece.
-John Ruskin

Day 17 __/__/__

Forgive, not forget. It's never easy to forgive and forget. But forgiveness is as much for you, as it is for your transgressor. Name one person you need to forgive and why.

Day 18 __/__/__

Becoming a Better Friend. What traits do you need to develop to become a better friend? Scratch out a quick list here:

There is nothing on this earth more to be prized than true friendship.
-Thomas Aquinas

Day 19 __/__/__

Dear Me, there are a lot of things you might know now that you wish you knew back then. Pen a letter of advice to your younger self.

Day 20 __/__/__

Relaxation Has a Rhythm. Music has the power to soothe the senses. List your ultimate relaxation playlist below.

One good thing about music; when it hits you, you feel no pain.
-Bob Marley

Day 21 __/__/__

A Delectable Diary. What are all the things you had to eat today?

Day 22 __/__/__

Something to smile about. What made you smile today? Make a list of all the things that brought you happiness today.

A warm smile is the universal sign of kindness.
-William Arthur Ward

Day 23 __/__/__

Not even money can buy... Money can't buy everything. What are three things that you can't live without, that don't come with a price tag?

Day 24 __/__/__

Scent-sational Days! It could be your favorite fragrance or just a scent that makes your heart sing. Describe your favorite scent-sations.

Nothing brings to life again a forgotten memory like fragrance.
-Christopher Poindexter

Day 25 __/__/__

Billionaire Behavior. Feeling lucky? Scratch out a quick list of the first ten things you would do if you became a billionaire.

Day 26 __/__/__

Keep the Clouds Away. Not everyone likes rainy weather – but it has its merits. What's your favorite thing about a rainy day?

Some people walk in the rain, others just get wet.
-Roger Miller

Day 27 __/__/__

Kitchen Keepsakes. What's your famous recipe? Create a kitchen keepsake for your family to use in the future by writing down your world-famous (to-be) recipe. Don't forget to add pictures if you have any!

Day 28 __/__/__

Nervous Notes. Make a note of what makes you nervous, and how you can get over it.

Great things never came from comfort zones.
-Unknown

Day 29 __/__/__

Your own super-power! What's one super-power you wish you had, and why?

Day 30 __/__/__

On your bookshelf. Name the last book you read, and share the most memorable part of it.

A reader lives a thousand lives before he dies.
-George R.R. Martin

Day 31 __/__/__

January's Scorecard. This was one heck of a month. Write down all the successes you achieved this month, no matter how small.

Day 32 __/__/__

Decoding your Dreams! Waking up from a dream can go one of many ways. Sometimes, we immediately forget everything we dreamt about, or we wake up haunted by something so real, it couldn't have just been a dream. Let's bring that dream from night to day – give a quick recount of your last dream here and answer the questions that follow.

What did you dream about?
What were you thinking about before you went to bed?
How would you feel if this dream came true?

If you can dream it, you can do it.
-Walt Disney

Day 33 __/__/__

What's Worrying You? Is something sticking you in the side? A worry you can't shake? Maybe writing it down will help you to figure it out. Jot down a list of all the things worrying you right now…and then ask yourself, is this something you can fix?

Day 34 __/__/__

Unplanned Magic. The best moments in our lives are sometimes the ones we don't plan. Remember an unplanned moment that turned out really well? Here's your chance to put it in writing.

Keep some room in your heart for the unimaginable.
-Mary Oliver

Day 35 __/__/__

Getting Down to Business! Perhaps there's an entrepreneurial spirit living inside you – here's one way to find out. Make a note of at least five (5) business ideas you would try, if you had the chance.

Day 36 __/__/__

Snack Time! Out with the chips, fries, ice cream and all your favorite snacks that come served with a side of guilt. Scan the internet for a quick, healthy snack recipe that's just your style and make a copy it down here. Don't be afraid to get creative – make it and even put your own twist on it. Snap a quick pic of the finished product and paste it here for a yummy addition.

Let food be thy medicine, and medicine be thy food.
-Hippocrates

Day 37 __/__/__

Photography List. Have an eye for great photos? Make a quick list of ten things to photograph today and start making memories with your phone or camera today.

Day 38 __/__/__

If you had more time in the day, you would… 'I don't have enough time to do this…' is a phrase more common than you could imagine. But what would you do if you had more time in the day? List at least three activities you'd like to do that don't quite fit into your 24-hour allotment.

Beware the barrenness of a busy life.
-Socrates

Day 39 __/__/__

What are ten things you can do to beat boredom? Write them down...then go do at least one.

Day 40 __/__/__

Free Yourself from Your Fears! Know what's mightier than the sword? That's right – the pen. So write your fear in the you-know-what right here. Then, see if the following questions can help you figure out how to beat it.

Why are you afraid?
What has this fear prevented you from doing?
Would you try counseling to get rid of this fear?

The fears we don't face become our limits.
-Robin Sharma

Day 41 __/__/__

What's in your bag? Are you carrying around unnecessary baggage? Empty out your handbag and make a list of all the contents. Then, beside each, write down whether each is 'Necessary' or serves 'No Purpose'. Your handbag could be lighter when you're through with this list!

Day 42 __/__/__

Never have I ever... Have a load of 'nevers' on your list? Things you've never done, places you've never been and lines you'd never cross...write down as many of them as you can think of.

Never regret. If it's good, it's wonderful. If it's bad, it's experience.
-Unknown

Day 43 __/__/__

Here's to all the firsts... Remember your first kiss? Your first car? Your first everything? These are the things that usually give us the ability to appreciate what we have now. Jot down a list of your 'firsts' and let's see just how far we've come.

Day 44 __/__/__

And the award for best decision ever goes to... Ever made a decision that you're really proud of? Well, that could be one for the books.

Don't base your decisions on the advice of those who don't have to deal with the results.
-Unknown

Day 45 __/__/__

A Little Self Love. Forget the chocolates, the roses and stuffed bears. This Valentine's Day, just love yourself and all the gifts you were born blessed with. Make a list of your favorite things about yourself.

Day 46 __/__/__

Who's your favorite person? There's a special room in your heart for this person. Who are they and why are they your favorite?

**The chances you take, the people you meet, the people you love, the faith that you have.
That's what's going to define you.**
-Denzel Washington

Day 47 __/__/__

A letter to _____ If you could write a letter to anyone (living or dead), who would it be? Put pen to paper and write to them what's in your heart.

Day 48 __/__/__

Lie Tracker. Whether it's a little white lie or a giant kaleidoscope, hold yourself accountable. What's one lie you've told recently?

A single lie discovered is enough to create doubt in every truth.
-Unknown

Day 49 __/__/__

Purge Period. No one likes to admit if they're a hoarder. But here's a start – compile a quick list of all the things you have that could better serve someone else and contact a local charity to make a donation.

Day 50 __/__/__

Tear-Jerkers. What are three things that always make you cry? Jot down your top tear-jerkers here.

Crying doesn't indicate that you're weak. Since birth, it's always been a sign that you're alive.
-Unknown

Day 51 __/__/__

Someone I'd like to meet. If you had the chance to meet anyone in the world, who would it be? Better yet…if you had the chance to talk to them, what would you say?

Day 52 __/__/__

Strangely Scrumptious! Some food combinations are just down-right strange; but for you, nothing's more delicious. What are your favorite unlikely pairings?

After a full belly, all is poetry.
-Frank McCourt

Day 53 __/__/__

One small change. If you could change one thing about yourself, what would it be and why?

Day 54 __/__/__

Here's to Good Hair. Everyone has bad hair days, but this one was the worst! Describe the worst hairstyle you've ever worn – if for nothing else, this will remind you to never do it again.

I think that the most important thing a woman can have (next to talent), is her hairdresser.
-Joan Crawford

Day 55 __/__/__

I'm blessed because... It's easy to overlook some everyday blessings when we have troubles. But it all comes down to perspective. List at least three things you are blessed with today.

Day 56 __/__/__

Becoming a Better Lover. Relationships are all about compromise. What are some of the things you could compromise on to make your relationship work better?

No relationship is perfect. There are always some ways to bend, to compromise, to give something up in order to gain something greater...
-Sarah Dessen

Day 57 __/__/__

There's an expert in the house! Everyone is really good at something. Make a list of at least five (5) things you could drop some knowledge on.

Day 58 __/__/__

I can't live without… Aside from some good ol' oxygen, what are some of the things you believe you can't live without?

Time, like money, is measured by our needs.
-George Eliot

Day 59 __/__/__

Wasn't this a lovely month? Make a quick assessment of the best things that ever happened in 28 days and scratch them down here.

Day 60 __/__/__

Extra Time! Mention at least 10 things you'd jump at the opportunity to do, if they ever came up.

Sometimes your only available transportation is a leap of faith.
-Margaret Shepard

Day 61 __/__/__

A Job for Someone Else. What are some of the tasks in your life that you wish you could hire someone else to do?

Day 62 __/__/__

The Next Best Thing Since Sliced Bread… Make a list of at least ten inventions you wish existed and why.

The measure of a man is what he does with power.
-Plato

Day 63 __/__/__

Dream Date. Describe the perfect date – from start to finish – with the person(s) of your dreams.

Day 64 __/__/__

A Self-Description. Imagine if you could see yourself through someone else's eyes...how would you describe you?

People seldom change. Only their masks do. It is only our perception of them and the perception they have of themselves that actually change.
-Shannon L. Alder

Day 65 __/__/__

The Most Important Promise. We all break promises from time to time – it's human nature. Become better at your promises by making one to yourself. Don't forget to hold yourself to it either!

Day 66 __/__/__

Just for Me! Everyone deserves to be pampered. Doesn't mean you should always wait on someone else to do it for you. Plan a personal day for yourself and make a list of all the most relaxing things you'll do.

If your compassion does not include yourself, it is incomplete.
-Jack Kornfield

Day 67 __/__/__

Nobody Has to Know. You know that part in the interview when they ask, 'What's something nobody else knows about you?'. Start practising your answer – jot down at least five things that no-one else knows about you.

Day 68 __/__/__

Unfinished Business. Sometimes we start things we just never get to finish – either because we don't have the time or we lose interest. Break this bad habit – list some of the things you've started but never finished, and see if you can go back and tick at least one (1) of these off your list of un-finished things to do.

Can anything be sadder than work left unfinished? Yes, work never begun.
-Christina G. Rossetti

Day 69 __/__/__

The Object of Your Admiration. Who do you admire, and why?

Day 70 __/__/__

Did Your To-Do List Get Done? Ever feel like you spent all day working but got nothing done? Make a list of all the things you did today –this could give a true picture of what you actually achieved.

What keeps me going is goals.
-Muhammad Ali

Day 71 __/__/__

If I ruled the world… Adjust your crown, queen. Should you be given the chance to rule the world, what ten things would be done in your reign?

Day 72 __/__/__

Not your average book report… Do you remember the last book you read? Scribble down the best things you got from it.

A book is a gift you can open again and again.
-Garrison Keillor

Day 73 __/__/__

What makes you happy? Know those things that make you smile, warm your heart and gives you the fuzzy feeling all the way in your soul? Make a list of them.

Day 74 __/__/__

Spring Fling. What are your favorite things about Spring?

No matter how long the winter, spring is sure to follow.
-Proverb

Day 75 __/__/__

The Best Food Ever! Was it the food that captured your heart? The ambience? The service? Capture the best moments from an unforgettable gastronomical experience here.

Day 76 __/__/__

A Friend to the End. If you could still be friends with one person from school (whether it's kindergarten or college), who would it be, and why?

Friends are the siblings God never gave us.
-Mencius

Day 77 __/__/__

Retail Therapy. What's the last thing(s) you purchased and why?

Day 78 __/__/__

In another life… At some point in your life, you may have harbored dreams of being something else. If you weren't doing what you do now, what would you have become, and why?

If you can't stop thinking about it, don't stop working for it.
-Unknown

Day 79 __/__/__

The Best Surprise Ever! You'll probably never forget this moment as long as you live…but just in case, you should write it down.

Day 80 __/__/__

A Do-Over. If you had the chance to take back something you said or did, what would you do differently?

Look forward with hope, not backwards with regret.
-Unknown

Day 81 __/__/__

The Chore of Choice. Admit it…you secretly love washing dishes…or something similarly domestic. What household chore is your favorite, and why?

Day 82 __/__/__

The Finance Nix-List. Whether it's always shopping hungry or your emotional 'treat yourself' default, what are some of the bad financial habits that you need to nix?

Money is not the only answer, but it makes a difference.
-Barack Obama

Day 83 __/__/__

The No-Eat List. These things will never venture past your lips. Ever.

Day 84 __/__/__

The Most Important Person in My Life. Who holds the top spot on your personal totem pole...your numero uno?

If you have only one smile in you, give it to the people you love.
-Maya Angelou

Day 85 __/__/__

Not your business, but... There's someone out there who could use your advice...but you're not one to go poking your nose in business that's not yours. But what if the advice you'd give is really good? Try seeing how it looks on paper first.

Day 86 __/__/__

A Dreamy Dessert. What's in the dessert of your dreams? Jot down the ingredients here.

Life is uncertain. Eat dessert first.
-Ernestine Ulmer

Day 87 __/__/__

The Role of a Lifetime. What are your role model's most attractive traits, and why?

Day 88 __/__/__

Currently…

I'm listening to _____
I'm reading _____
Planning a trip to _____
Breaking the habit of _____
Learning how to _____
Eating _____
Drinking _____
Pretending to _____
Ignoring _____
Wanting _____

Change the game, don't let the game change you.
-Macklemore

Day 89 __/__/__

Confidence. What gives you confidence?

Day 90 __/__/__

Nailed it! You're doing even better than you know. Drop a quick list of all the things you've done really well this month and how you feel about them.

Your positive action, combined with positive thinking, results in success.
-Shiv Khera

Day 91 __/__/__

This Month's Scoreboard! There must have been at least thirty-one awesome things about March. See how many you can recall.

Day 92 __/__/__

Movie Moments. What's one movie you can recite by heart, and why?

Movies are so rarely great art that if we cannot appreciate great trash, we have very little reason to be interested in them.
-Pauline Kael

Day 93 __/__/__

The Soundtrack of Your Childhood. Can you even remember the soundtrack of your childhood? Jot down a list of your favorite music from the good old days.

Day 94 __/__/__

Hope Floats. What gives you hope?

Never lose hope, my dear heart. Miracles dwell in the invisible.
-Rumi

Day 95 __/__/__

Something to Celebrate! Every week may not be good, but there must be a list of good things in every week. What's yours?

Day 96 __/__/__

Impossible Dreams. Everyone tells you it's impossible, but that's never stopped you from dreaming. Use this opportunity to scribble down even your most impossible-sounding dreams. You'd never know — that might be the first step towards making them come true.

Impossible only means they haven't found the solution as yet.
-Unknown

Day 97 __/__/__

Morning Rituals. Describe your morning ritual step-by-step. Is there anything you would change?

Day 98 __/__/__

Too sweet to beat. Rank your favorite desserts in order from 10 to 1, with 10 being the most scrumptious!

Every once in a while, a girl has to indulge herself.
-Sarah Jessica Parker

Day 99 __/__/__

Hair I am. List all the hairstyles you've ever experimented with – the good, the bad, and the ones-you-wish-you-could-forget.

Day 100 __/__/__

Your reading list. What's on your reading list for April?

A room without books is like a body without a soul.
-Cicero

Day 101 __/__/__

On the Clock. What's your favorite time of day, and why?

Day 102 __/__/__

The Day Ahead. Every day is an opportunity to become better than you were yesterday. You can start by setting at least three short-term goals for tomorrow. On your mark, get set, go-al!

You should set goals beyond your reach so you can always have something to live for.
-Ted Turner

Day 103 __/__/__

What Inspires You? We all have a quote, scripture or saying that we reach for when we're running low on inspiration or motivation. List as many of yours as you can below.

Day 104 __/__/__

A New View. Look out the window and make a note of all the different things you notice.

It's not what you look at that matters, it's what you see.
-Henry David Thoreau

Day 105 __/__/__

Flashback. Ever wondered how much you'd grow? Think back to exactly where you were and what you did this time last year.

Day 106 __/__/__

Rewriting Your Own Fairy Tale. Imagine yourself the heroine of your own fairy tale. What roads would lead to your happily ever after?

Life itself is the most wonderful fairy tale.
-Hans Christian Anderson

Day 107 __/__/__

A letter from your own worst enemy! Not everyone's going to be your fan, that's just a part of life. But are you doing something to earn yourself more enemies than allies? Try putting yourself on the other side of the fence—what if you were your own worst enemy…? What missive would you pen to yourself?

Day 108 __/__/__

Baggage Check! Sometimes, we harbor negative feelings in our hearts and our minds are weighed down by grudges we've forgotten how they started in the first place. Before you journey into a new day, confiscate that baggage yourself. Make a list of all the things you'd be better off if you let go.

Once you replace negative thoughts with positive ones, you'll start having positive results.
-Willie Nelson

Day 109 __/__/__

A Map of Your Heart. Whip up a quick list of all your favorite places in the world, and your best memory of each.

Day 110 __/__/__

Missing You... Who do you miss?

Perhaps one day we will meet again as characters in a different story, maybe we'll share a lifetime then.
-Pavana

Day 111 __/__/__

Hindsight is 20/20. Some things you wish you knew before-hand; they would have made life so much easier. Make a list of all the things you wish you had known five (5) years ago.

Day 112 __/__/__

What Excites You? The signs are always evident – your breathing gets shorter, heart beats faster, palms get sweaty and goosebumps cover every square inch of your skin! What are the things that get you excited?

Her lips were drawn to his like a moth to a flame.
-Anya Seyton

Day 113 __/__/__

Memorable Meals. Just thinking about it now has you salivating…what was your most memorable meal this week?

Day 114 __/__/__

Can I Have a Genie in a Bottle, Baby? Everyone wishes they had three wishes…what are yours?

Where there is great love, there are always wishes.
-Willa Cather

Day 115 __/__/__

Getting in the Habit of Good Habits! Name a good habit you'd like to start today.

Day 116 __/__/__

A Hard Pill to Swallow? Criticism is not always easy to take – we puff up, take it personally and miss the point more often than not. What were the last bits of criticism you received, and how did you respond?

The only way to avoid criticism: do nothing, say nothing, and be nothing.
-Aristotle

Day 117 __/__/__

I knew you were trouble when you walked in… Admit it, some people you'd be better off not knowing. Right? Who are some of the persons you wish you'd never met, and why?

Day 118 __/__/__

What's under the bed? For as long as you can remember, there are just some things that have always sent you scuttling under a blanket, into your mom's bed at midnight covered in the heebie-jeebies and the unexplainable scare-ables. What are you afraid of, and why?

Courage is resistance to fear, mastery of fear, not absence of fear.
-Mark Twain

Day 119 __/__/__

Long-Term Living. Where do you see yourself in five years...? ...ten years down the line? Will you be in the same career? Plans like these should start from early – so write down at least five long-term goals.

Day 120 __/__/__

Style Settings. Is it the blue cashmere sweater over your best pair of worn-in jeans? Or perhaps your grandma's vintage bomber jacket with a pleated miniskirt? Drop a quick list of your top style picks below.

Style is a way to say who you are without having to speak.
-Rachel Zoe

Day 121 __/__/__

This Month's Scoreboard! A month has passed since we last did this! What did this month teach you?

Day 122 __/__/__

Time Bomb. What if you only had one month to live...how would you spend each day?

To live is the rarest thing in the world. Most people just exist.
-Oscar Wilde

Day 123 __/__/__

Build-A-Best-Friend. Aside from being a 'ride-or-die', what other top qualities do you look for in a bestie?

Day 124 __/__/__

Rules were meant to be broken… Do you stop at every single stop sign and toe the chalk line? Didn't think so either. What are some of the rules you've broken, you little rebel you…!

Learn the rules like a pro, so you can break them like an artist.
-Pablo Picasso

Day 125 __/__/__

Adulting 101. When you're a kid, you can't wait to grow up and do all the things grown-ups can. But things can get tough when you're an adult and have to fend for yourself. With no-one to kiss your boo-boos and tuck you in at night, what do you think are some of the worst things about being 18 and over?

Day 126 __/__/__

Matinee Time. What are your top ten movies to watch this month?

Creativity is a wild mind, and a disciplined eye.
-Dorothy Parker

Day 127 __/__/__

Choices, Choices, Choices! Would you prefer to be able to fly or to read minds?

Day 128 __/__/__

Birthday Magic. You still talk about it to this day…that's how good it was. Which of your birthdays was absolutely unforgettable and why?

Life should not only be lived; it should be celebrated.
-Osho

Day 129 __ / __ / __

Trending. What are your favorite trends of the past decade?

Day 130 __ / __ / __

Golden Circle. Only a few really make it into our closest social circles. Who's in yours?

There are friends, there is family, and then there are friends that become family.
-Unknown

Day 131 __/__/__

A Taste of Success. Some weeks can be really trying. List at least 5 things you've learnt since the week started.

Day 132 __/__/__

Become a better sister. You could really be a better sister by making these five changes:

A sister is a gift to the heart, a friend to the spirit, a golden thread to the meaning of life.
-Isadora James

Day 133 __/__/__

It was a dark and stormy night... When it's raining cats and dogs and you're trapped inside where it's warm and dry, what are you favorite go-to activities to beat the weather blues?

Day 134 __/__/__

Living Fiction. Imagine you could exchange lives with a fictional character...who would you choose?

Truth may be stranger than fiction, but fiction is a lot more interesting.
-A.J. Race

Day 135 __/__/__

The world could use more… Go on…write what you think the world needs more of!

Day 136 __/__/__

Are you living the life you planned? Have you started achieving the goals you set for yourself many years ago? Are you where you thought you'd be in life right now?

Dream as if you'll live forever, live as if you'll die tomorrow.
-Unknown

Day 137 __/__/__

What's holding you back? Is there something that keeping you from achieving your goals and making your dreams come true? See if you can put your finger on it and pop it right down below.

Day 138 __/__/__

Random Acts of Kindness. It doesn't take much to be kind. List ten ways that you can be kind to someone in the next few days…and make it happen!

Kind words can be short and easy to speak, but their echoes are truly endless.
-Mother Theresa

Day 139 __/__/__

Dungeon Decisions. Imagine you've found yourself stuck in a dungeon. What's your plan of action?

Day 140 __/__/__

Life Lessons. As a child, parents often turn into our enemies when they serve punishment for a misdemeanor. What are some of the punishments you received as a child that taught you something? And which of these will you be passing on to your own children?

Mistakes are portals of discovery.
-James Joyce

Day 141 __/__/__

Dear Future Me... What are some of the thing you want your future self to know?

Day 142 __/__/__

Living Outrageously. Ever did something so outrageous, you startled even yourself? Jot it down.

Courage is like a muscle; it is strengthened by use.
-Ruth Gordon

Day 143 __/__/__

Celeb Crush. Whose poster would you kiss?

Day 144 __/__/__

Lesson Plan. Every day is an opportunity to learn something new. What are some of the things you'd like to learn?

The capacity to learn is a gift; the ability to learn is a skill; the willingness to learn is a choice.
-Brian Herbert

Day 145 __/__/__

TV Guide. Can't decide what to watch? Drop your top ten favorite TV shows below.

Day 146 __/__/__

Time Machine. If you could go back in time and change anything, what would that be and why?

Blessed are the curious, for they shall have adventures.
-Lovelle Drachman

Day 147 __/__/__

Dealing with Disappointment. What's the most disappointed you've ever been? Make a note of what caused this.

Day 148 __/__/__

School Days. What was your favorite subject in school and why?

Education is the key to unlock the golden door of freedom.
-George Washington Carver

Day 149 __/__/__

Sleep tracker. Sleep helps your body to recuperate and rest. Are you meeting you sleep goals? Why or why not?

Day 150 __/__/__

Complimentary behavior. Drop the best compliments you've ever received right here.

True humility is being able to accept criticisms as graciously as we accept compliments.
-Sabrina Newby

Day 151 __/__/__

Matters of Health and Heart. What are your health goals? Jot them down below. Don't forget to add some reasonable and realistic target timelines to keep yourself accountable.

Day 152 __/__/__

This Month's Scorecard. Fun times this month, right? What did you enjoy doing the most?

If you can't stop thinking about it, don't stop working for it.
-Unknown

Day 153 __/__/__

A Time to Shine. What are some of your proudest moments, and why?

Day 154 __/__/__

No longer a stranger. Who is the last person you met? Describe them in full detail.

Remember that every good friend was once a stranger.
-Unknown

Day 155 __/__/__

Dear future kids… Write a letter to your future kids with at least 3 key points of wisdom you want them to live by.

Day 156 __/__/__

Summer Daze. Summer is arguably one of everyone's favorite seasons. What makes it awesome for you?

If The summer night is like the perfection of thought.
-Wallace Stevens

Day 157 __/__/__

Comedy Central. What are some of the funniest moments you've ever experienced?

Day 158 __/__/__

Procrastination Situations. Procrastination is said to be the thief of time. What did you procrastinate about getting done this week, and why?

Procrastination is, hands down, our favorite form of self-sabotage.
-Alyce P. Cornyn-Selby

Day 159 __/__/__

Daily Motivation. What motivated you to get going this morning?

Day 160 __/__/__

Eat your words? Ever encountered someone who never believed in you? What would you tell them if you saw them today?

Not all words fit to their meanings. Sometimes what is said is not what is meant and what is meant is left unsaid.
-Unknown

Day 161 __/__/__

Holiday Fever. What's your favorite holiday, and why?

Day 162 __/__/__

Experts Wanted! You could be an expert at anything…but what would you choose, and why?

We're all experts in our own little niches.
-Alex Trebek

Day 163 __/__/__

Cultural Conversations. All cultures are unique in their own right...but what makes you proud about yours?

Day 164 __/__/__

Measuring Mistakes. Everyone makes mistakes; it's a very human thing to do. What are some of the biggest mistakes you've ever made and what did you learn from them?

Mistakes are the stepping stones to success.
-John C. Maxwell

Day 165 __/__/__

The Perfect Day. Does it start with sunshine and sunny-side eggs? Describe your perfect day below — don't leave out a single minute.

Day 166 __/__/__

It's All Relative. Is it Aunt Rosie or Uncle Joe? Describe your favorite relative here and why they mean so much to you.

I think togetherness is a very important ingredient to family life.
-Barbara Bush

Day 167 __/__/__

Shipwrecked! You're trapped on a desert island (you know the story); What happens next?

Day 168 __/__/__

Saying No to Negativity. Plagued by negative thoughts? Remove them from your heart and leave them on the page.

Negativity is a thief; it steals happiness.
-Unknown

Day 169 __/__/__

Dance Playlist. Dance party for one? What songs make it on the playlist?

Day 170 __/__/__

Dear future soulmate... Sometimes, you need to have an idea of what you're looking for in a soul-mate. Jot down the top ten attributes you'd find appealing.

Our soulmate is the one who makes life come to life.
-Richard Bach

Day 171 __/__/__

Dream Living. If you could live anywhere in the world, where would it be, and why?

Day 172 __/__/__

Terrifying Times. What were some of the most terrifying experiences of your life?

If you want to conquer fear, don't sit at home and think about it. Go out and get busy.
-Dale Carnegie

Day 173 __/__/__

Toy Story. Do you remember your favorite rag doll? Or was it a stuffed animal? Which toy stole your heart as a child?

Day 174 __/__/__

Tomorrow's Goals. What three things would you like to achieve tomorrow?

A goal should scare you a little and excite you a lot.
-Joe Vitale

Day 175 __/__/__

Healing the Heart. Based on your own life experience, what advice would you give to someone dealing with a broken heart?

Day 176 __/__/__

Belief kills…and cures. What do you believe in?

P Man is made by his belief. As he believes, so he is.
-Johann Wolfgang von Goethe

Day 177 __/__/__

You-topia. What's your idea of Utopia?

Day 178 __/__/__

The Queen's Questions. If you were granted an audience with the Queen (of wherever), what ten questions would you definitely ask?

Curiosity is the wick in the candle of learning.
-William Arthur Ward

Day 179 __/__/__

Childhood Memories. What were the best parts of your childhood?

Day 180 __/__/__

Pros and Cons. List three bad things that happened today, and three good ones.

Extremes are easy. Strive for balance.
-Colin Wright

Day 181 __/__/__

A word for This Month. If you could sum up this last month in one word, it would be
_____.

Day 182 __/__/__

If you were a cat… …what would be at the top of your agenda?

Cats are connoisseurs of comfort.
-James Herriot

Day 183 __/__/__

Fashion is forever. Rank your top ten fashion trends ever.

Day 184 __/__/__

No regrets? If today was your last day on earth, what would you regret never having done?

Fear will pass, but regret lasts forever.
-Unknown

Day 185 __/__/__

Matinee Moments. What was the last movie you saw, and what was your favorite part?

Day 186 __/__/__

What's in a name? Do you know the meaning of your name? It might take a bit of research but see what you come up with.

If I'm gonna tell a real story, I'm gonna start with my name.
-Kendrick Lamar

Day 187 __/__/__

Noise pollution. What sounds annoy you?

Day 188 __/__/__

Summer Reading. Which books are on your summer reading list?

In the end, we'll all become stories.
-Margaret Atwood

Day 189 __/__/__

A Speech for Your Haters. You get five minutes to address an audience made up entirely of people who hate you. What would you say?

Day 190 __/__/__

Self-Love. What is your favorite body part, and why?

You alone are enough. You have nothing to prove to anyone.
-Maya Angelou

Day 191 __/__/__

How it used to be... Not everyone can deal with change. Name one adjustment you've had to deal with recently and why you wish you could return to the way it was before.

Day 192 __/__/__

Your favorite failure. That time you failed, but learnt the most valuable lesson ever.

If you learn from defeat, you haven't really lost.
-Zig Ziglar

Day 193 __/__/__

Message in a Bottle. What if you could send a message to a stranger in a bottle across the ocean. What would your note say?

Day 194 __/__/__

Vacation Time. Ready to plan that vacation to _____? Let's go! Pick a place from your bucket list and start planning a real-life trip, down to what you'll be packing in your bag.

Laughter is an instant vacation.
-Milton Berle

Day 195 __/__/__

Summer Schedule. What are 20 things you must do this summer? Even if it's just to go read a book in the park or try out the sorbet shop on the corner, what's on your schedule?

Day 196 __/__/__

Alone Time. List at least 10 activities to do when you're all by yourself.

Loneliness is the poverty of self; solitude is the richness of self.
-May Sarton

Day 197 __/__/__

Trends to the End. Make a list of all the trends you just wish never, ever, ever, ever existed. Ever.

Day 198 __/__/__

Rejection. No-one likes being rejected. Can you remember a time you were rejected? How did it make you feel? How did you recover?

Rejection is God's protection.
-Alice Hunt

Day 199 __/__/__

Misery Loves Company Music. Feeling sad? Quickly jot down your somber song selections.

Day 200 __/__/__

Time to Forgive Yourself. Holding a grudge against yourself is one of the toughest things to do. What are you finding it hard to forgive yourself for?

Forgive yourself for your faults and your mistakes and move on.
-Les Brown

Day 201 __/__/__

Strong Points. What are five of your key strengths?

Day 202 __/__/__

Forecast. Describe today's weather and how it's impacting your mood.

If you want to see the sunshine, you have to weather the storm.
-Frank Lane

Day 203 __/__/__

Unsaid Words. Ever said something you wish you could take back?

Day 204 __/__/__

Tomorrow… Here are all the reasons tomorrow will be better than today:

The best thing about tomorrow is that it comes one day at a time.
-Abraham Lincoln

Day 205 __/__/__

Shopping List. Three things you must buy ASAP because…

Day 206 __/__/__

Texts for your Ex. All the things you ever wanted to tell your ex, write it here. It will save you the late-night drunken rants…if you're into that kind of thing.

Don't stress the could haves. If it should have, it would have.
-Unknown

Day 207 __/__/__

Trust Issues. Who do you trust the most? ('Yourself' doesn't count)

Day 208 __/__/__

Values and Valuables. What is the most expensive thing you own, and why is it important to you?

A fool knows the price of everything and the value of nothing.
-Unknown

Day 209 __/__/__

Socially Acceptable. What's the last social gathering you attended, and what was your favorite part of it?

Day 210 __/__/__

Shame on You! Your most embarrassing moment goes a little like this...

Your mistakes do not define you.
-Psalm 37:24

Day 211 __/__/__

When you woke up today... Who was the first person you thought of, and why?

Day 212 __/__/__

The Gift of Giving. Do you remember the last time you gave someone a gift? What was it, and why was it special?

A kind gesture can reach a wound that only compassion can heal.
-Steve Maraboli

Day 273 __/__/__

Not Getting Your Way. Whether you throw a tantrum or slink away into the shadows, how you react to not getting your way speaks volumes about your maturity and selflessness. Do some reflection—how do you react when you don't get your own way?

Day 274 __/__/__

Hit restart. Which day do you wish you could take back and restart, and why?

Every new beginning comes from some other beginning's end.
-Seneca

Day 275 __/__/__

Legacy. When you leave this world, how will you be remembered? More importantly, how do you want to be remembered?

Day 276 __/__/__

Here's to all the kind people! Raise a written toast to all the people in the world who you've seen spreading kindness.

What wisdom can you find that's greater than kindness?
-Jean Jacques Rousseau

Day 217 __/__/__

What's troubling you? That chip on your shoulder must be a heavy cross to bear. Offload it unto these pages and see if you feel any lighter.

Day 218 __/__/__

Read Between the Lies. Over-reacting is a normal human behavior. Sometimes, however, it can be totally uncalled for. Can you recall a situation where you overreacted unnecessarily about something that could have been avoided if you had just read between the lines?

It's not our stress that kills us, it is our reaction to it.
-Dr. Hans Selye

Day 219 __/__/__

A Time of Sadness. Life is all about balance – some days you'll be happy and others, not so much. Quickly jot down a brief description of one of the saddest moments you've experienced.

Day 220 __/__/__

Crazy Cravings. If you could have anything you desire for dinner today, what would it be?

Desire is craving enough to sacrifice for.
-Myles Munroe

Day 221 __/__/__

Myself as a Poet... Do you think in limericks and rhymes? Drop a few lines about something that means a lot to you.

Day 222 __/__/__

A Body of Problems. Whether it's your big nose or your thin lips, your knocked knees or your bushy eyebrows, we all have that one body part that's like the stepchild of the body. What's your and why do you hate it?

Be happy with what you have, while working for what you want.
-Helen Keller

Day 223 __/__/__

What I learned today… What are ten tiny things you learned throughout today?

Day 224 __/__/__

The Search for Balance. For every bad thing that happened today, find two good ones.

Life is a balance of holding on and letting go.
-Rumi

Day 225 __/__/__

A cuppa this... Coffee or Tea? Why?

Day 226 __/__/__

Picture This. Picture yourself a painter. Compile a list of all the things you would paint in a week and do at least one.

Art is the journey of a free soul.
-Alev Oguz

Day 227 __/__/__

Favorite Fictional Characters. Who are your favorite made-up characters and why?

Day 228 __/__/__

Your last meal. If you had only one meal remaining on this earth, what would you eat and why?

It is not death than a man should fear, but he should fear never beginning to live.
-Marcus Aurelius

Day 229 __/__/__

Evening Rituals. Describe your evening rituals and share which part of your evening ritual you just can's skip and why.

Day 230 __/__/__

Unforgettable Advice. There is some advice that sticks with us like lifetime guardian angels, keeping us from making the same mistake twice. What are some of the best pieces of advice you've ever received?

Many receive advice, only the wise profit from it.
-Publilius Syrus

Day 231 __/__/__

Fearing the Future. The future is something to look forward to, but we all have fears. What makes you worry about the future? List your fears here.

Day 232 __/__/__

Theme Song. It's everything about who you are in a song…you know, like the 'Fresh Prince' or 'The Power Rangers'. What would be your theme song? None measure up? Write your own, then!

Life is one grand sweet song, so start the music.
-Ronald Reagan

Day 233 __/__/__

Missed the Lift? Sometimes, opportunity knocks and the doors open, but we just never got to go in. Jot down all the missed opportunities in your life, and why.

Day 234 __/__/__

Dismissing Hatred. When you hate someone, you technically keep them in your heart and mind. You have to remember you hate them and hate them with a lot of energy sometimes. Make some space in your heart and clear them out of your mind – who do you hate and why?

Hate has caused a lot of problems in this world, but it has not solved one yet.
-Maya Angelou

Day 235 __/__/__

Happy Fingers. What cheers you up when you are down? Make a list here.

Day 236 __/__/__

Dreamy Views. You just moved into your dream home and you look through the kitchen window. Describe the view in detail.

Dreams are the touchstones of our character.
-Henry David Thoreau

Day 237 __/__/__

Sharing the Good News. You get some really good news. Who's the first person you tell, and why?

Day 238 __/__/__

The Unforgivables. There are just some things you'd never be able to overlook, much less forgive and forget. What are those?

Let us forgive each other – only then will we live in peace.
-Leo Nickolaevich Tolstoy

Day 239 __/__/__

Chef Me! What's your specialty? Drop the recipe down below and share how you learnt to make this dish/drink.

Day 240 __/__/__

Your secret desires. From the bottom of your heart, these are the things you'd like to do the most. This is a no-judgement zone, so feel free to note your secret desire(s) here and why you want to do them so badly.

The starting point of all achievement is desire.
-Napoleon Hill

Day 241 __/__/__

Things I'd Do If I Weren't Afraid. Fear ever made you miss out on something? That's understandable. Make a list of all the things you'd do if you weren't afraid.

Day 242 __/__/__

Passionista. We all have something that we're passionate about. What's yours, and why?

Be fearless in the pursuit of what sets your soul on fire.
-Unknown

Day 243 __/__/__

This Month's Scoreboard. How many good days/bad days did you have this month? Which was more, and why?

Day 244 __/__/__

Healthy Choices. Whether its drinking a healthy smoothie or running in the park, what are five healthy choices you've made so far this year, and how are the results looking?

Health is not valued until sickness comes.
-Thomas Fuller

Day 245 __/__/__

Sorry Count! List the last ten things you apologized for, and why.

Day 246 __/__/__

Hope. What do you hope for the most this month?

Where there is no vision, there is no hope.
-George Washington Carver

Day 247 __/__/__

You time! A day at sea or a day hiking in the mountains. Which would do you more good, and why?

Day 248 __/__/__

The Behavior Audit
Remember a time you mistreated someone? Who was it and how do you feel about your behavior towards them? Have you done anything to make it right or do you think they deserved it?

What wisdom can you find that's greater than kindness?
-Jean Jacques Rousseau

Day 249 __/__/__

Overcoming betrayal. Remember the times you felt most betrayed and jot them down here.

Day 250 __/__/__

Taking Credit. A colleague at work takes credit for a great project you did. What do you do?

Never stop doing your best just because someone didn't give you the credit you deserve.
-Unknown

Day 251 __/__/__

Expressing Creativity! What are ten things you can do to get your creative juices flowing?

Day 252 __/__/__

Three 'Wise Men' or More. Who are the wisest people you know personally, and what make you think that? Drop their phone numbers and email addresses here too, and get in touch with one of them today.

Science is organized knowledge. Wisdom is organized life.
-Immanuel Kant

Day 253 __/__/__

Trying New Things. So many new things to try! What five things are at the top of your list?

Day 254 __/__/__

Making Sacrifices. What are ten (10) sacrifices you've had to make in your life, and what were the reasons?

True success requires sacrifice.
-Rick Riordan

Day 255 __/__/__

Someone to See More Often. Name someone you need to start seeing more often, and why.

Day 256 __/__/__

Animal Instinct. Which animal do you relate to the most, and why?

Animals share with us the privilege of having a soul.
-Pythagoras

Day 257 __/__/__

Paying for Preference. Would you prefer to do a job you love for very little pay, or a job you hate with a huge salary? Why?

Day 258 __/__/__

Blowing off Steam. What are you mad about? Do a little heart cleansing – drop them in a list here.

Those who are at war with others are not at peace with themselves.
-William Hazlitt

Day 259 __/__/__

Loving Life. What are the three best things about your life?

Day 260 __/__/__

Priorities. List today's priorities in order from 1-10, with '1' being the most important.

If you chase two rabbits, you will not catch either one.
-Russian Proverb

Day 261 __/__/__

Aboard the Hardship. It would have tested your limits, broken your heart and run you ragged, but you're still here shining in your strength and ability to survive. What are the hardest things you've ever had to go through?

Day 262 __/__/__

A Burst of Energy. Do you know those things that when you do them, you start feeling like you can take on the world? Yeah? Make a list of ten (10) things that energize you.

The energy of the mind is the essence of life.
-Aristotle

Day 263 __/__/__

Comfort Foods. Is it a yummy plate of mac and cheese? Or a tub of cookie-dough? List your favorite comfort foods below and share when you feel the urge to draw for them.

Day 264 __/__/__

Hobby Hut. What are the things you enjoy doing the most, and why do they bring you joy?

Happy is the man who is living by his hobby.
-George Bernard Shaw

Day 265 __/__/__

Where Does My Money Go? What do you spend your money on? Draw a pie chart to show how you spend your money monthly and see if there are any adjustments you can, or need to make.

Day 266 __/__/__

Signs of the Zodiac. This one may take a little research...does your zodiac sign match your personality? Share your findings down below.

Be yourself, everyone else is taken.
-Unknown

Day 267 __/__/__

Picnic Feast. You've been designated the food-basket-packer-person for an upcoming picnic. What's going to make it into your basket, and why?

Day 268 __/__/__

Beautiful Places. Describe the most beautiful place you've ever been, and don't leave out a single detail.

Everything has beauty, but not everyone sees it.
-Confucius

Day 269 __/__/__

Bully Encounters. Remember that time you had to encounter a bully? Share your experience here.

Day 270 __/__/__

My Own Movie! There's going to be a movie made about your life. Who will play your character, and why?

Only I can change my life. No one can do it for me.
-Carol Burnett

Day 271 __/__/__

Foot-in-Mouth Situation! List three (3) times you found yourself with your foot in your mouth, and how you got out of it.

Day 272 __/__/__

Favorite Weekend Routines. How do you spend your weekends, and why? Does it make you feel happy and rested?

Rest and be thankful.
-William Wordsworth

Day 273 __/__/__

Retirement. How would you like to spend your golden years?

Day 274 __/__/__

I said, 'No'. Make a list of all the times you remember saying 'no' to something. Did you make the right choice?

My goal now is to remember every place I've been, only do things I love and not say yes when I don't mean it.
-Sandra Bullock

Day 275 __/__/__

New Hobbies. Add something new to your résumé of hobbies…list three new things you'd like to try, and why.

Day 276 __/__/__

A Prayer of Thanks. Let's say thanks for all the good times this month.

If the only prayer you say is thank you, that would be enough.
-Meister Eckhart

Day 277 __/__/__

Not all heroes wear capes... Who is your personal hero, and why?

Day 278 __/__/__

Today's Silver Linings. List at least three (3) good things that happened today.

Too many people miss the silver lining because they're expecting gold.
-Arthur Yorinks

Day 279 __/__/__

100 candles. If you lived to see 100, how would you spend your birthday and why?

Day 280 __/__/__

How do you see life? Optimist, Pessimist or Realist…which of these best describes you, and why?

Deep in their roots, all flowers keep the light.
-Theodore Roethke

Day 281 __/__/__

Talent Inventory. Make a list of all the talents you have, no matter how small or how unusual.

Day 282 __/__/__

Less is more. What's one thing you have a lot of in your life, but could do with less?

Less is more only when more is too much.
-Frank Lloyd Wright

Day 283 __/__/__

Positive Affirmations! Words have the power to motivate and inspire. What are three (3) of your favorite affirmations?

Day 284 __/__/__

Breast Test. When was the last time you did a breast examination? There are so many websites and videos online that could show you step-by-step. Check them out and write your own steps for doing it to share with a friend this month.

When life kicks you, let it kick you forward.
-Kay Yow

Day 285 __/__/__

The one who knows me best. We all have at least one person who knows us and understands the way we are better than anyone else in the world. Who is that, and how did they learn so much about you.

Day 286 __/__/__

Power of Prayer. List all the things you've ever remembered praying for. Do you have any of those things now?

Prayer is the cure for a confused mind, a weary soul and a broken heart.
-Unknown

Day 287 __/__/__

Self-Care. What are some of the things you can do or habits you can start practising to take better care of yourself? Is it a new skincare regimen? A spa day?

Day 288 __/__/__

Unfulfilled Childhood Dreams. Do you have an unfulfilled dream from your childhood? Is it something you could make come true, either for yourself or a child?

Shoot for the moon, and if you miss, you'll be among the stars.
-Les Brown

Day 289 __/__/__

A Job to Dream About! In your dream job, what do you spend your days doing?

Day 290 __/__/__

What Makes You Mad? Try to remember the last few times you got mad. What caused it, and why?

Anger begins with madness, and ends with regret.
-Imam Ali

Day 291 __/__/__

Daily Inspiration. Make a list of all the things that inspired you today.

Day 292 __/__/__

Values. List three important personal values, and why they mean so much to you.

When your values are clear to you, making decisions becomes easier.
-Unknown

Day 293 __/__/__

I Scream for Ice Cream. Ice cream comes in many flavors. But if you had your way, this flavor would be a reality, and here's why:

Day 294 __/__/__

Morning Motivation. What motivated you to get out of bed this morning?

It always seems impossible until it's done.
-Nelson Mandela

Day 295 __/__/__

A little recklessness. What was the last most reckless thing you did, and why did you do it?

Day 296 __/__/__

Room for Improvement. List some of the things you've improved on this year.

Practice the philosophy of continuous improvement. Get a little bit better every single day.
-Unknown

Day 297 __/__/__

Somewhere to Hide. What was your favorite hiding place as a child, and why?

Day 298 __/__/__

Pain. What's the most pain you've ever felt, and how did you get over it?

What hurts us is what heals us.
-Paulo Coelho

Day 299 __/__/__

Evening Rituals. What do you look forward most to doing when you get home in the evenings?

Day 300 __/__/__

Funny Bone. Life's too short to take everything seriously. So list all the funniest things that happened this week, and laugh at them one more time.

If love is the treasure, laughter is the key.
-Yakov Smirnoff

Day 301 __/__/__

Something to sip on... Whether it cools you down, perks you up or just quenches your thirst, what are your favorite things to drink, and why?

Day 303 __/__/__

Colorful. It's your favorite color – and these are all the things and places that you can find it in.

The soul becomes dyed with the color of its thoughts.
-Marcus Aurelius

Day 302 __/__/__

Birthplace. Where were your born? And when's the last time you were back there?

Day 304 __/__/__

Understanding Your Points of Weakness. Whether it's things you're not good at or things you're just not able to do, take stock of all your weaknesses in a list below.

Sometimes you don't realize your own strength until you come face to face with your greatest weakness.
-Susan Gale

Day 305 __/__/__

Innocent Games. We can never forget some of the games we played as a child, because they gave us such innocent fun. What were some of your favorite games, and why?

Day 306 __/__/__

This Month's Scoreboard. What are three stressful things you experienced this month, and how did you overcome them?

Stressed spelled backwards is *desserts*.
-Loretta Laroche

Day 307 __/__/__

On my way to school. How did you get to school when you were a child? Start from as early as kindergarten.

Day 308 __/__/__

Motivation. Make a list of at least ten things that motivate you.

Try and fail, but don't fail to try.
-John Quincy Adams

Day 309 __/__/__

What Hurts You. Make a list of all the things that have ever hurt you, physically or emotionally.

Day 310 __/__/__

Laughter Triggers. It starts in your ears, and then travels down to your funny bone before spreading all over your body…make a list of all these things. And if you don't know where to start, think of all the things that have ever made you laugh and write them down right here.

Life is full of happiness and tears; be strong and have faith.
-Kareena Kapoor Khan

Day 311 __/__/__

Mo' Money, No Problems. If money were no object, how would you spend today?

Day 312 __/__/__

Disliking Yourself. Name three character traits that you have, and why you despise them.

Comparison is an act of violence against the self.
-Iyanla Vanzant

Day 313 __/__/__

The Most Important Love Letter. Dear me, I love you because…Pen a doting love letter to yourself, highlighting all the reasons you love you!

Day 314 __/__/__

Arguments. What was the last argument you had, with whom and why? Has the issue been resolved?

Be calm in arguing, for fierceness makes error a fault and truth discourtesy.
-George Herbert

Day 315 __/__/__

A Place to Live. Would you prefer a home by the ocean or high up in the mountains? Why?

Day 316 __/__/__

Social Affairs. What social issues are you passionate about, and what are you doing about them?

Friends are medicine for a wounded heart, and vitamins for a hopeful soul.
-Steve Maraboli

Day 317 __/__/__

Revenge. What was the last thing you took revenge for? Did you feel vindicated?

Day 318 __/__/__

These hands that build. Have you ever built or made anything from scratch? What was it and how did you do it?

Creativity is the way I share my soul with the world.
-Brene Brown

Day 319 __/__/__

Apologies. To all the people you owe apologies, let's write them an IOU. Who deserves an apology from you, and why? Take it up a notch by hand-delivering at least one.

Day 320 __/__/__

Helping Friends! Make a list of all the ways you can help someone this week—no matter how simple.

We rise by lifting others.
-Robert Ingersoll

Day 321 __/__/__

Justifying Jealousy. Who have you ever been jealous of, and why?

Day 322 __/__/__

Shopping for Talents! What if you could multiply all your talents? Make a list of all the new talents you hope to nurture and become good at.

Talent can't be taught but it can be awakened.
-Wallace Stegner

Day 323 __/__/__

Things I Care About. Compile a list of twenty things you care about…and why you do.

Day 324 __/__/__

Paid in Compliments. Have you paid anyone a compliment lately? Start practising – what are some things you could compliment people on?

Verbal compliments, or words of appreciation, are powerful communicators of love.
-Gary D. Chapman

Day 325 __/__/__

Childhood Bliss. What gave you complete and utter happiness as a child?

Day 326 __/__/__

Favorite TV Advertisement. Whether it made you laugh or it touched a personal chord with you, what's your favorite ad, and why?

An idea can turn to dust or magic, depending on the talent that rubs against it.
-Bill Bernbach

Day 327 __/__/__

Gift List. In your book, who's been naughty or nice. Make a list of these persons, and what you'll be getting them for the holidays.

Day 328 __/__/__

What would you do if… You just got married and your partner gets offered a dream job in a country thousands of miles away. You just got a promotion yourself and wouldn't be able to join them until a year later. What would you do?

Distance is just a test to see how far love can travel.
-Unknown

Day 329 __ / __ / __

Ten-Year-Old Pride. Name something you did today that would have left your ten-year-old self in awe.

Day 330 __ / __ / __

Thank you! Write down the last ten times you remember saying 'thank you' and what it was for.

No duty is more urgent than that of returning thanks.
-James Allen

Day 331 __/__/__

Lost and Found. If someone should find this journal many years later, what would be your message to them? Write this page, rip it out and stick it at the front of this journal.

Day 332 __/__/__

Purpose. Everyone was put on earth for a purpose. What do you think yours is?

The meaning of life is to find your gift. The purpose of life is to give it away.
-Pablo Picasso

Day 333 __/__/__

Personal Qualities I Admire. Each of your friends have at least one quality you admire. Jot down their names and the quality you admire the most.

Day 334 __/__/__

Skin Care. Write your skin care routine step-by-step, as though you're teaching someone else how to do it. Don't have one? Do a bit of research, write the steps down and start today!

An empty lantern provides no light. Self-care is the fuel that allows your light to shine brightly.
-Unknown

Day 335 __/__/__

This Month's Scoreboard! Write down all the successes you achieved this month, no matter how small.

Day 336 __/__/__

Time to Purge. Make a list of all the things you need to purge from your life, before the New Year comes. Whether it's a pair of old boots you never wear that's taking up space in your closet, or a pair of jeans that cost too much when you bought it so it brings you grief and guilt when you think about throwing it away.

Nothing is more invigorating than cleansing your mind of old thoughts and inventing fresh ones to ponder and act upon.
-D. Russell

Day 337 __/__/__

Your Go-To Style. Every woman has at least one killer outfit that knocks the socks off everyone who sees them. What's yours? Feel free to snip from magazines and online photos to support your style.

Day 338 __/__/__

Winter Wonderland. Make a list of all your favorite things about the season.

Adopt the pace of nature; her secret is patience.
-Ralph Waldo Emerson

Day 339 __/__/__

Last Laugh. Who was the last person to make you laugh, and what did they do or say?

Day 340 __/__/__

Overcoming Fears. What is one thing that you use to be afraid of, but it doesn't scare you anymore?

Never let your fear decide your future
-Unknown

Day 341 __/__/__

Taking Risks. When was the last time you took a risk? Was there a reward at the end of it?

Day 342 __/__/__

A Letter to Santa... Pen a quick letter to Santa sharing all your wishes for the holiday season.

No one has ever become poor by giving.
-Anne Frank

Day 343 __/__/__

The Nice List. Have you been good this year? Write all the reasons why you should be on Santa's nice list this year.

Day 344 __/__/__

Daily Motivation. List at least 5 things that have motivated you this year.

Difficult roads often lead to beautiful destinations.
-Unknown

Day 345 __/__/__

Wrong Kind of Profile. Can you think of at least one time when you were racially profiled? What happened and how did it make you feel?

Day 346 __/__/__

A Higher Being. Do you believe in a higher being? Why or why not?

All things are possible for those who believe.
-Mark 9:23

Day 347 __/__/__

Get Me Bodied. If only your nose was a little more…or your eyes were another color…or your legs a little longer…which body parts would you change if you could, and why?

Day 348 __/__/__

Helping Hands. Make a list of all the times you can remember someone helping you with anything.

The smallest deed is better than the greatest intention.
-John Burroughs

Day 349 __/__/__

A Winner's Dinner. You're at a table with all your favorite people who are home for the holidays. Who are these people and what are you having for dinner?

Day 350 __/__/__

Moody Hues. Use a color to describe your mood right now and say why.

Colors are the smiles of nature.
-Leigh Hunt

Day 351 __/__/__

The Best Things Ever. Make a list of all your bests so far this year:
Best Day (and why)
Best Song
Best Outfit
Best Book I've Read
Best Movie I've Watched
Best Meal I've Eaten
Best Lesson I've Learnt
Best Compliment I've Received
Best Achievement
Best Memory
Best Joke I've Heard

Day 352 __/__/__

Today's failure. Name one thing you failed at today, and what you've learnt from it.

Failure is a part of success
-Hank Aaron

Day 353 __/__/__

Dream Mate. If you could get married to anyone in the world, who would it be, and why?

Day 354 __/__/__

Sticks and Stones. Can you remember the meanest thing anyone has ever said to you? How did you respond? If you could replay that moment, what else would you say?

Do not let their words grieve you.
-Surah Yunus

Day 355 __/__/__

Traditions. Make a list of your favorite family or holiday traditions.

Day 356 __/__/__

Today feels like... Jot down all the words you could possibly use to describe today.

What you do today can improve all your tomorrows.
-Ralph Morrison

Day 357 __/__/__

New Traditions. What are some of the traditions you've changed or created in your own family, and why?

Day 358 __/__/__

Gift Hall of Fame. Hands down, this is a list of the best gifts you've ever received and the awesome givers who gave them to you.

It's not the gift, but the thought that counts.
-Henry Van Dyke

Day 359 __/__/__

A Mistake I Never Want to Make Again. Because only once is it a mistake…if you do it again, it becomes a choice, right?

Day 360 __/__/__

Another year of opportunity. What are your major goals for next year?

Success is where preparation and opportunity meet.
-Bobby Unser

Day 361 __/__/__

Lessons from Last Year. This year has been quite a teacher. What were some of her best lessons?

Day 362 __/__/__

The Honor Roll. Here's to all the goals we've achieved! Jot down your big (and small) accomplishments for this year…and hey, a pat on the back is in order.

The way to get started is to quit talking and begin doing.
-Walt Disney

Day 363 __/__/__

This Month's Scoreboard. What are you thankful for this month?

Day 364 __/__/__

Precious Gifts. List the most precious moments you have experienced throughout the year. Yup, those you'll probably never forget.

A good life is a collection of happy moments.
-Denis Waitley

Day 365 __/__/__

Anniversary!

It's official. It's been a year since we started this little habit! List down 5 ways your life has been impacted by this journal. It may be time to pick up another one!

Keep a daily diary of your dreams, goals, and accomplishments. If your life is worth living, it's worth recording.
-Marilyn Grey

~~End~~

To New

Beginnings...

Notes

Notes

Notes

Notes

Notes

Notes

Notes

Notes

Notes

Notes

Notes

Notes